John Ruskin, Frederick Startridge Ellis, Thomas James Wise

Stray Letters from Professor Ruskin to a London Bibliopole

John Ruskin, Frederick Startridge Ellis, Thomas James Wise

Stray Letters from Professor Ruskin to a London Bibliopole

ISBN/EAN: 9783337429157

Printed in Europe, USA, Canada, Australia, Japan

Cover: Foto ©ninafisch / pixelio.de

More available books at **www.hansebooks.com**

SOME STRAY LETTERS

OF

PROFESSOR RUSKIN.

STRAY LETTERS

FROM

PROFESSOR RUSKIN

TO

A LONDON BIBLIOPOLE.

1892.

London: Privately Printed

(Not for Sale.)

CONTENTS.

CONTENTS.

CONTENTS.

CONTENTS.

PREFACE.

CHARACTER and genius. like murder,
"will out." The gentleman to whom
the following letters are addressed was
for some years in frequent business
relations with Mr. Ruskin, as will be
readily seen from the tenour of many of
the letters. But that these are no mere
dry business missives the reader of a
few pages taken at random will promptly
discover. It is not, indeed, in the
nature of Mr. Ruskin to keep up a
correspondence, even concerning what
he desires to buy, and what he no
longer needs and therefore wishes to
sell. without entering upon side issues

and explaining motives. Hence we
obtain, in this primarily business correspondence, glimpses of his views concerning the method of publication
proper for his own adoption, and on
the genius of Sir Walter Scott; of his
opinions upon Thomas Carlyle and
Mr. Mallock; and, above all, overflow-
ings of that geniality and good-hearted-
ness, which all who know his nature
will expect. If the letters are too
slight to be offered to the general
public, they are too pregnant to be
allowed to remain in the complete
seclusion of the manuscript state; and
the editor of this little volume is much
beholden to Mr. Ellis for his dis-
interested kindness in allowing his
letters to be printed.

LETTERS.

NOTE.

The following letters were addressed to Mr. F. S. Ellis, sometime of New Bond Street, now resident at Torquay. They are but the remnant of a much more considerable correspondence,—the main part having been given away at various times to autograph-collecting friends.

Some of the dates are only approximate, having been inserted from memory after a lapse of years.

PROF. RUSKIN'S
LETTERS TO F. S. ELLIS.

— ·✕· —

LETTER I.

— --

Corpus Christi College,
Oxford.
February 17th, 1870.

Dear Mr. Ellis,

Will you please send me to Denmark Hill the best recent edition of Vasari (the largest print of original better than many notes), and the best translation also. I am terribly nervous about chance of misreading anything.

Ever truly yours,

J. Ruskin.

LETTER II.

DENMARK HILL,
LONDON, S.E.
February 25*th.* 1870.

DEAR MR. ELLIS,

Would you kindly look out for me a copy of Le Normand and De Witte's work on Greek vases.   You must get me one from Paris, if one is not to be had in London.

The Vasaris are very nice ; I'm so glad you were interested about them.

I hope illustrations to *Paradise* may get done at last.*

Tennyson is quite fallen—he must be ill.

Ever most truly yours,
J. RUSKIN.

* A projected edition of Morris's *Earthly Paradise*, with illustrations by Burne Jones—a project hitherto unfulfilled.

LETTER III.

GENEVA,
May 5th, 1870.

DEAR MR. ELLIS,

My assistant did quite right in availing himself on my part of your courteous permission to return the De Witte,* if unsatisfactory; his judgment is quite enough for me. Will you inform the French house that the book is for the Art Gallery of Oxford, and cannot be placed there if ill-executed. Let the plain copy be sent without binding, as I wish to arrange and bind it myself.

Most truly yours,

J. RUSKIN.

Mr. F. S. Ellis.

* See the previous letter.

LETTER IV.

DENMARK HILL,
LONDON, S.E.
[1871.]

DEAR MR. ELLIS,

Can you get me Sir I. Newton's tract on Daniel?

I am greatly pleased with that book of portraits that Mr. Green found for me,—and the edition* of *Tale of a Tub* is nice.   Can you find out for me, anyhow, if there was an analysis of *Fors Clavigera* in the *Guardian?*

Truly yours,

J. RUSKIN.

---

* A copy of the First edition of Swift's *Tale of a Tub*.

LETTER V.

CORPUS CHRISTI COLLEGE,
OXFORD.
August 25th, 1872.

DEAR MR. ELLIS,

Please get me the enclosed, and send
it with the other books bought yester-
day, and the Ottley, when obtained, all
together down to

        Brantwood,

              Coniston,

                    Lancashire,

which will now be my address per-
manently.

        Ever gratefully yours,

                J. RUSKIN.

I want also Lavoisne's *Chronological
and Geological Atlas*, Barfield, Wardour
St., 1822, if obtainable.

LETTER VI.

BRANTWOOD,
CONISTON, LANCASHIRE.
September 19th, 1872.

DEAR MR. ELLIS,

I find I want the 1st and 2nd vols. of the *Earthly Paradise.* I had them complete at Oxford, but only my two last vols. here.

Thanks, so much, for explanation about Savonarola.

Tell me how Mr. Green is?

Any effect produced on customers' minds yet by our burnt sacrifice? *

---

* The enquiry is a jest—the story is this. Mr. Ruskin saw in Mr. Ellis's possession a fine copy of *Capriccios de Goya* (a Spanish artist, 1746—1828), and justly commented on its hideousness, adding that "it was only fit to be burnt." Mr. Ellis agreed with him; and putting the volume into the empty grate (for it was in August), he and Mr. Ruskin set light to it, and the book was burned to ashes.

Also the best modern French Dictionary, and Kingsley's book on heroes.

Also the oldest, if attainable, and the best, not modern, edition of (Italian) Vasari.

Ever truly yrs.,

J. RUSKIN.

LETTER VII.

BRANTWOOD,
CONISTON, LANCASHIRE.
January 3rd, 1874.

My DEAR ELLIS,

I am greatly delighted with your letter because, as far as I can guess, it lets me hope you really can come down *just now ;* and I am in a state of disquiet with myself from having nobody else to speak to, which will make it a special charity to me if you will,—the rather that there are very few people whom I would ask ; many of my best friends having angles, which get into my ribs and hurt me, when we are living together. But I particularly want you to come, because I think you will enjoy a wintry day or two (as many as you can spare, please) in the extreme quiet of this place, and you always help and never hurt me.

If this thaw holds, travelling will be as safe as usual to-morrow ; and if you can tell me what day you can come, I will send a carriage for you to the Windermere Station, which you can easily reach now by daylight. I will write however to-morrow what trains are best. I can't ascertain to-day, for they change (probably) at the New Year, and I haven't got the new time-bill.

Ever very gratefully yours,

J. RUSKIN.

LETTER VIII.

BRANTWOOD,
CONISTON, LANCASHIRE.
January, 1874.

MY DEAR ELLIS,

Saturday will do delightfully for me. I trust the weather may be a little in better humour for you also.

How good of you to go to the "tea-shop";* and I'm so glad of your report, and must really get up my signs.

Ever most truly yours,

J. R[USKIN].

---

* This was the "tea shop" near Wigmore Street, where Mr. Ruskin started two of his mother's old servants in business. (See *Fors Clavigera,* Nos. 48 and 67.)

LETTER IX.

ROME.
June 3rd, 1874.

MY DEAR ELLIS,

I had your kind note, and am heartily glad you were able to get the books for my young and old lady friends.

I have been taking a course of Emile Gaboriau to acquaint myself with modern Paris: he seems to me to have a wonderful knowledge of the town and its evils. As specimens of its average middle class literature, these novels— generally beginning with a murder, and having some form of theft, or delicate form of adultery, for principal subject—all through, are highly curious. But from all I see and read we are advancing faster to revolutions, and miseries of the horriblest kind, than I ever dreamed ; and I have not taken a cheerful view of matters this many a day. This Italy is in an unspeakably fearful and perilous state.

My Oxford men * can, I hope, bear being laughed at. They are the only sane ones I know of—but I wish I had seen the correspondence about them.

Ever yours most truly and obliged,

J. RUSKIN.

Kind regards to Mr. White.

My address is : *Poste restante*, Assisi.

* " My Oxford men " ; *i.e.* some undergraduates (Mr. Ruskin's disciples at Oxford) who, about the date of the letter, had undertaken to make a roadway through the hamlet of Hincksey, near Oxford—upon Mr. Ruskin's suggestion that they should apply their physical strength to something yielding a tangible result. The " correspondence " referred to was simply some letters in the newspapers (as silly as usual) on the subject.

LETTER X.

— —

DENMARK HILL,
LONDON, S.E.
November 2nd, [1874.]

DEAR MR. ELLIS,

The *Somville* * has come, and is delightful.

If *I* saw my way clearly to everything but the binding, I should not be much troubled about *that.* But of course it " must be thought on."—I wish we were ready for it.

However, I am fairly at work. I have resolved to take Chaucer's *Dream* instead of *The Flower and the Leaf,* and I think I can make a very pretty and

---

* A French book on Art.

useful introduction to everything out of it.*

Ever most truly yours,

J. RUSKIN.

F. S. Ellis, Esq.

---

* This refers to a series of early English reprints, to be furnished with Introductions by himself, which Mr. Ruskin at that time contemplated publishing through Mr. Ellis. His suggestion that *The Flower and the Leaf* is not now esteemed to be by Chaucer caused the change. Unfortunately the same difficulty applies to Chaucer's *Dream*.

LETTER XI.

DENMARK HILL.,
LONDON, S.E.

[1874.]

DEAR MR. ELLIS,

Will you please find and send me the best authoritative edition of Chaucer.* I don't mean an early expensive edition, even if you could find one ; but the best modern one, what anybody wishing now to read Chaucer would be obliged to put up with. Also, I am perpetually referred in mine to " Du Cange." I don't know who " Du Cange " is, but I want him, please. †

Yours most truly,

J. RUSKIN.

* There was no "authoritative" edition of Chaucer in 1874—and there is not one to-day.

† Du Cange *Glossarium ad scriptores mediæ et infimæ latinitatis,* 7 vols. 4to.

LETTER XII.

DENMARK HILL,
LONDON, S.E.

[1874.]

DEAR MR. ELLIS,

My woodcutter* is, I am sorry to say, too busy to take more work just now, except only for *Earthly Paradise.* —I will let him work on that.

Ever most truly yours,

J. RUSKIN.

---

* Mr. Arthur Burgess, whom Mr. Ruskin employed extensively, believing him to be the only skilful wood engraver to be found at the time. Mr. Ruskin wrote a lengthy article upon Burgess and his work in *The Century Guild Hobby Horse* for *April*, 1887. Mr Ellis had asked, and obtained, Mr. Ruskin's consent for him to work upon the projected illustrated edition of *The Earthly Paradise*, but he never did anything for it.

LETTER XIII.

KIRBY LONSDALE.
Thursday, January 25th, 1875.

MY DEAR ELLIS,

You never did me a greater kindness than in sending me these books to look at.   I suppose they are far beyond my power in price,—and for that matter the songs * I should not care to have, and even the Hogarth † would be a horror in the house.   But yet I couldn't part with them before I had to come away, they were full of such intense interest to me.

I never had seriously studied Hogarth before,—and he and Fielding pull so splendidly together, stroke and bow.

* **A** collection of seventeenth century broadside ballads.
† A collection of Hogarth's prints in various states.

The songs entirely justify what you said; but you see they have one quality—to me a very redeeming one—perfect naturalness and *openness*, while in modern literature every fine passage of sentiment is liable to have a lurking taint in it. At least, these ballads would do *me* not the least harm, while Tennyson's *Vivien* would do me much. —However, I feel rather knocked down, on the whole, by them.

May I keep them till I go back? If you want them they can be sent up at any time (for I left them packed ready for sending) if you wanted them.

The Children's books ‡ are—what you said. But I've kept all but one, with best thanks for your trouble.

The *worst* I consider Christina Rossetti's. I've kept that for the mere wonder of it!—how she could—or

‡ A number of children's books, which Mr. Ruskin had requested Mr. Ellis to procure for him.

Arthur Hughes—sink so low after their pretty nursery rhymes !

Oh dear—*how* I wish you had been at breakfast this morning at Brant-wood !

Did the Ferns behave well at all ?

Please don't forget, or change your mind, about coming in spring with Mrs. Ellis.   You *must* see the view from my window yet.*

Always faithfully   and   gratefully yours,

J. RUSKIN.

I'm posting up to Oxford.   A line would find me at Post Office, Wakefield.

---

* During the whole of Mr. Ellis's previous visit, in *January* 1874, a fog hung persistently over the lake.

LETTER XIV.

ARTHUR SEVERN'S;
                HERNE HILL,
                        LONDON, S.E.
                                [1875.]

MY DEAR ELLIS,

So many thanks for your kind letter,
and sending to Birmingham, &c. Yes,
please get me that Italian economic
book.*

I must keep the *publishing* of the
Notes † with Allen, not to break the
public impression of my obstinacy ; but
if you would endure the trouble and
petty worries of letting them be sold
from your counter, you should have

---

* An old Italian book on the *Monti di pietà*.
† *Notes on the Principal Pictures in the Royal
Academy*, No. vi., 1875.

them exclusively in London. No I
can't say that, neither—for if other
booksellers wanted them I could not
refuse ; but I will take no measures for
regular sale except from your counter,—
if you will allow it.

They'll be out next week, very early
I hope.

Ever affectionately yours,

J. RUSKIN.

May I put, on title—" G. Allen,
Sunnyside, and F. S. Ellis, 29, New
Bond Street " ?

LETTER XV

—————

AYLESBURY.
May 26th, 1875.

MY DEAR ELLIS,

I am very glad to have been brought here at this moment;—the hawthorn, and buttercups with clover, purple and gold, being beyond anything I ever yet dreamed of in England ; and the walks through it all so heavenly.

By enclosed note you will see that if I allow £20 per 1,000, or £2 per 100, I am well guarded as to cost. Then if you give me £3 10*s.* for the hundred, we have both 30 per cent.— which seems to me pleasant and fair? And you can do just as you please about the booksellers, none shall have any but you and Allen.

Mrs. Severn is greatly amused by playing at agency, and has taken orders for 50 or so. She is to have 100,—the first parcel of them sent. Other sendings you can order from Jowett * at your own pleasure, but I am still uneasy at the idea of the trouble you will have for so small a matter.

I think *Fors* for June, though delayed for a day or two, won't be a bad one ; for the biography, simple though it be, amuses me myself as it comes into my head, and the correspondence tickles me.

Always faithfully yours,

J. RUSKIN.

* The Manager at Messrs. Watson and Hazell's printing works at Aylesbury.

LETTER XVI.

AYLESBURY.

[*May* or *June*, 1875.]

MY DEAR ELLIS,

It's immensely good of you under-
taking the book together with Allen.
I've ordered the title-page, with double
publisher, by this post. *Such* a bother
as the thing has been to me ;—one can't
see the pictures for the crowd, and I
miss some, and over-rate others, again
and again. But there's a nice spicy
flavour in it now, I think—as a whole—
quite a " loving cup " for the Academy.
I get my full revise to-morrow, and send
for press on Monday. You will have
all you want sent you on the same
terms as Allen ; and please, offer it in

any way you think best to the other booksellers, and to the public—only don't advertise in newspapers.

Gratefully yours,

J. R[uskin].

LETTER XVII.

GEORGE INN,
AYLESBURY.
[*June*, 1875.]

DEAR ELLIS,

Notes ready, price 1s. I hope to be sent on Friday.—Can't tell the trade price till to-morrow, but it will be reasonable, I doubt not. The thing is bigger than I meant—fifty-six pages.*

Mr. Jowett, Printing Works, Aylesbury, will receive all directions from you. I'm here till Friday.

Ever faithfully yours,

J. R[USKIN].

---

* As a matter of fact the pamphlet consists of fifty-nine pages.

LETTER XVIII.

———

[George Inn,
Aylesbury.
June, 1875.]

My Dear Ellis,

At the last moment I discover two
fatal mistakes * in my last sheet of
Notes, and must cancel it, and you
can't have them now till Tuesday.   In
case you get your packet, mind you
send none out ; but I hope I've stopped
them.   They'll be ready on Tuesday.

Ever gratefully yours,

J. R[uskin].

* Merely misprints, to rectify which the sheet was
cancelled.

LETTER XIX.

[LONDON.]
June 27th, 1875.

MY DEAR ELLIS,

I wonder if I've by any chance lost a letter of yours, for I haven't had a single word since the *Notes* came out— and I expected some compliments !— and am disappointed ! Please send me just a little line, when you come home again, to Brantwood ; though I shan't be there till Wednesday week, I believe,— but they'll know where I am.

I left a packet of autographs (the refuse of that nice parcel, which seemed to me to spoil the rest) in Bond St. the other day. If they're the least use to anybody you can put them in auction,

or allów me for them ; if not, send them
to care of Arthur Burgess, 73 Mont-
pelier Road, Peckham, S. E.

Always affectionately yours,

J. R[uskin].

LETTER XX.

LICHFIELD.
June 30th, 1875.

MY DEAR ELLIS,

I have just seen an article in the *Telegraph* on Dr. Schliemann—the excavator in the Troad—which refers to his "autobiography." I am intensely desirous to see this, but fear there may be no translation.

Can you refer me to any completer account of the grand fellow than this absurd *Telegraph* one?

Write to Bolton Abbey.

Ever affectionately yours,

J. RUSKIN.

F. S. Ellis, Esq.

LETTER XXI.

--

BOLTON BRIDGE,
July 4th, 1875.

My Dear Ellis,

I am really *very* glad of your two delightful letters, this of *June 28th* only reaching me to-day—and being especially helpful to me in all ways, but chiefly in what you say of the short letter I wrote to *The World.* It is so very valuable to me in confirmation of errors which it has taken me long to make entirely definite even to myself, and which I feared would remain more than disputable to men actively engaged in business. It is this sympathy with my ways of thought which renders me always anxious to know if my books have given you pleasure.

K

Your letters to-day have brightened an already bright forenoon, the first fair one we have had on our journey; and a walk on the moorland, in the upper reach of Wharfdale, has given me more feeling of return to life than has come to me since those dark days which you helped me to bear patiently (except for your sake) at Coniston.

If at any time you like to follow my, really not unwise, example in this way of travelling, and bring Mrs. Ellis to Coniston to see our fine cascade, you would really find it little else than one delightful park-drive all the way, in the line I have taken—Oxford—Warwick —Lichfield—Ashbourne—Castleton— Wakefield—and here. There is nothing but the actual towns of Sheffield, Wakefield, and Leeds to pass of entire ugliness; the country is beautiful, even between Wakefield and Leeds; and the drive from Castleton commands one of the finest moorland views in England.

I shall certainly be at Coniston for two months from this time, and Mr. and Mrs. Severn would help me to make the visit as pleasant as we could for you both.

Ever faithfully and gratefully yours,

J. RUSKIN.

LETTER XXII.

BRANTWOOD,
CONISTON, LANCASHIRE.

July 23rd, 1876.

DEAR ELLIS,

Alas, I can give you too perfect satisfaction !

The *Loire* drawing, of which this oil is a copy, *was* mine, and *is* now at Oxford — where I gave it to the schools.

This copy ought to be traced. It is a dexterous and most criminal imitation.*

Ever yours in flying haste,

J. RUSKIN.

* This was a (probably) spurious Turner, which had been offered for sale to Mr. Ellis, in perfectly good faith, by a Mr. B— —, once a pupil of Mr. Ruskin's. Its origin was never traced, and Mr. Ellis declined to purchase it.

LETTER XXIII.

BRANTWOOD,
CONISTON, LANCASHIRE.
[*October 9th,* 1877.]

DEAR ELLIS,

I have never answered your kind letter of gentle remonstrance with me, for asking you to get what could not be gotten. But I am very glad to know the rarity of that old German Bible,* though I am very sorry for it, for its cuts are splendid,—nearly all, I believe, designed by Holbein ; and the Apocalypse cuts especially seem to me originals by Holbein, afterwards taken and enlarged by Dürer. But I forget all about the dates and relations

* The edition of Froschover, Basle, 1536.

I.

of these two men—and my days grow shorter and fewer, and I've no time to look.

You will be sorry to hear of a trouble I've had this last ten days, in Mrs. Severn's illness. The danger is past, her doctor says (and he is a good one, to whom I am profoundly grateful). But I've had a terrible fright, and feel now stunned a little, and giddy, and can't remember dates.

Please can you find for me Sedgwick's *Letters on Lake district?*

It is a lovely district to day; cloudless, and the lake* an expanse of boiling blue like the blue of ground ivy.

Kindest regards to Mr. White.†

Ever affectionately yours,

J. R[uskin].

* Coniston Water.
† Mr. White,—Mr. Ellis's business partner.

LETTER XXIV.

--- --

BRANTWOOD,
CONISTON, LANCASHIRE.
May 7th, 1878.

MY DEAR ELLIS,

I do not doubt your being pleased
to hear, from myself, that I have once
more dodged the doctors ; and hope,
henceforward, with Heaven's help, to
keep them out of the house,—at least
till I lose my wits again.* I'm picking
them up at present, here and there,
like the cock with the pomegranate
grains in the *Arabian Nights ;* which I
find just now my best "entertain-
ments"—after the spring flowers.

---

* See note at foot of p. 71 of *Letters upon Subjects of
General Interest from John Ruskin to various Corre-
spondents ;* London, privately printed, 1892.

These last have had no "doctoring,"
in my wood ; and grow—and do—as
they like exactly ; which I perceive to
be the intention of Providence that
they—and I—*should*, and propose to
follow their good example as I best
can. Above all, never to write any
business letters,—except when I want
to buy books, or missals ! You haven't
anything in that way, have you, to tell
me of ?

At any rate, will you please at once
set your Paris agents to look out for all
the copies that come up, at any sale,
of Rousseau's *Botanique* with coloured
plates, 1805—and buy all they can
get ; † which, on receiving (if ever a
kind *Fors* sends some) you will please
forward to Allen's forthwith, to be
kept in store for a St. George's Guild
school-book.

I'm not allowed to write letters

---

† Mr. Ellis was unable to obtain any copies of
Rousseau's *Botanique* - so far as his memory serves him.

by Joan* yet !—but shall coax her to let this one go, now it's written ; and am ever

Affectionately yours,

J. Ruskin.

Mind, this order for Rousseau is quite serious.　I am working on *Proserpina* steadily, and that edition is out and out the best elementary botany existing.

* Mrs. Arthur Severn

LETTER XXV.

BUCK INN,
MALHAM.
August 3rd, 1878.

DEAR ELLIS,

I was very heartily sorry not to see you again before leaving town, to assure you how much I was pleased with Jones's work, * and much else derivative from it, in the Grosvenor. I shall be compelled to disturb my peace among the hills here by giving Master Mallock† his pickle in next *Nineteenth Century*.

Will you kindly get this book for me, and send it here : *The Earth*, by

---

* Mr. Burne-Jones's *Golden Stairs*.
† Mr. W. H. Mallock, author of *The New Republic*, &c.

Elisée Réclus! and, if it is getable, I want a nice copy of James Forbes's *Travels in the Alps* sent to my godson Phil. Burne Jones, at the Grange.

Ever your affectionate

J. RUSKIN.

LETTER XXVI.

———

BRANTWOOD,
CONISTON, LANCASHIRE.
May 19th, 1879.

DEAR PAPA * ELLIS,

How are you? and what are you about? Cataloguing, or buying? You happy creature. And I hav'nt bought a bit of MS. this six months! and have left your account unpaid, hav'nt I? Please just send me brief word what it is, and I'll remit.

But I write to ask about enclosed gentleman's MS., which I left with you for your opinion. Can you give me

---

* This appellative originated from a remonstrance Mr. Ellis had addressed to Mr. Ruskin, on his declared intention of denuding himself of his entire fortune and property—an intention which appeared to be perfectly serious.

any price for it ?   If so, please write
to the owner, and make your offer.

And, I want a nicely bound edition
of Scott's mixed prose and poetry, if
there is one ; but especially of Paul's
Letters.

And, I shall have a great lot of old
books to sell, now I've done with
Oxford.   Would you manage it for
me ?

And I am always,

Your affectionate and obedient,

J. RUSKIN.

LETTER XXVII.

MY DEAR ELLIS,

I've been speechless with indignation since you let go that *Guy Mannering* MS.,* but suppose I must forgive *papa* Ellis,—especially since I want something of him !

Please, will you get me a good edition of *Julian the Apostate.* I find I've got to read him, at least a good lot of him, very carefully, before I can do a sentence more of *The Bible of Amiens !*

---

* The MSS. of Sir Walter Scott's *Guy Mannering* and *St. Ronan's Well* were sold by auction in 1881 ; but as they went for a higher price than Mr. Ellis considered they were worth, he would not buy them for Mr. Ruskin.

Gibbon quotes the Leipsic edition at the beginning of the 24th chapter (vol. iv. of my Gibbon). But *any* big print will do, and don't be long, for I'm dying to be at him.

Ever your much injured, but dutiful,

J. R[uskin].

LETTER XXVIII.

BRANTWOOD,
CONISTON, LANCASHIRE.
February 16*th*, 1881.

DEAR 'PAPA' ELLIS,

I've a particular reason for writing to you to day—especially because I am *really* angry with you for being so much of a Papa; and I have seen that you were quite right, and I'm entirely and deeply grateful to you. And yet I'm going to be as extravagant as ever at heart, but can't tell you now.

Ever your affectionate

JOHN RUSKIN.

LETTER XXIX.

BRANTWOOD,
CONISTON, LANCASHIRE,
February [1881].

DEAR PAPA ELLIS,

Why, am not I a "boy"?—and shouldn't I like to be more of one than I am! And I wish your old head was on my young shoulders.

What on Earth do you go missing chance after chance like that for! I'd rather have lost a catch at cricket than that *St. Ronan's*. Do *please* get it anyhow for me this once. I can't telegraph—the nasty people won't let me send a man—and—there's the bell ringing for dinner!

Seriously, my dear Ellis, I do want you to secure every Scott manuscript that comes into the market. *Carte blanche* as to price — *I* can trust *your* honour; and you may trust, believe me, *my* solvency. But I am deeply grateful for the more than kind feeling which checks you in our bids. Go calmly, but unflinchingly, in next time —and never fear, for

Ever your loving,

Son George.

LETTER XXX.

BRANTWOOD,
CONISTON, LANCASHIRE.
Tuesday, March 22nd, 1881.

MY DEAR PAPA ELLIS,

I have just found yours of date *Feb.* 17*th*,—which I suppose I must have packet away in a confused parcel of other things, just before a nasty attack of that overwork illness I had three years ago, came on again.

I'm well through it, I hope ; but the *St. Ronan's Well* MS. will be a wonderful balsam to my wounded soul, and more or less broken head.   Send it on instantly, if you've got it.   Of course I can trust my good old papa Ellis about price, &c.

Answer this, or please let Mr. White answer, to *me*, at once.

Ever your grateful and affectionate,

JOHN RUSKIN.

Hand shaky a little, *just yet*,—nothing wrong really with head or heart, thank God !

LETTER XXXI.

BRANTWOOD,
CONISTON, LANCASHIRE.
Thursday, March 24th, 1881.

DEAR PAPA ELLIS,

Your telegram last night gave me pleasant sleep; and your letter this morning, eager anticipation of the parcel by this afternoon's rail. There will be no question about my keeping the MS.,—but my reason for especially wishing to possess this one, is widely other than you suppose.

I cannot but confess myself much mortified that (whether as my papa, or my—may I say – admirer? in literary effort) Papa Ellis should never have read my classification of Scott's novels

P

in my essays on *Fiction* in the *Nineteenth Century!*

You will there see that *St. Ronan's Well* is marked as pre-eminently characteristic of the condition of clouded and perverted intellect under which Scott suffered, at intervals, ever since his first attack of gout in the stomach. These two attacks of *mine* have been wholly on the brain— and, I believe, conditions merely of passing inflammation. But the phenomena of the two forms of disease are intensely important to me, in relation to my future treatment of myself.

I am buying Scott's and other manuscripts, observe now, for my future Museum; and shall without hesitation add to the Scott series when any addition is possible.

Ever gratefully and
affectionately yours,
J. RUSKIN.

F. S. Ellis, Esq.

LETTER XXXII.

——————

BRANTWOOD,
CONISTON, LANCASHIRE.
March 25th, 1881.

MY DEAR ELLIS,

There is no doubt of my keeping the MS.,* unless I get sold up, books and all. It is more amazing to me than I can tell you to find it as steady as the others in the hand—even the part he had to re-write to please his accursed printer. I hope your box and *key* will come safe back to you.

Did you get a letter from me a month back, asking you to look out for a dainty old *Iliad*, of some good large type, for me?

* The autograph manuscript of one of Sir Walter Scott's novels—probably *Woodstock*.

Please, also, I want to know the best large type edition now extant of Carlyle's earlier books, — chiefly the *Past and Present*. Also of Richardson's *Clarissa ;* and of Miss Edgeworth's *Ormond* (or *Harrington and Ormond*), and *Helen*.

Ever your grateful " scapegrace,"

J. R[uskin].

LETTER XXXIII.

BRANTWOOD,
CONISTON, LANCASHIRE.
March 27th, 1881.

MY DEAR PAPA ELLIS,

I am more grateful than you could
at all believe for your thought for me.
I am so desolate in this world, that
the sense of any one's really watching
over me, and caring about me in a
useful way, is like balm and honey.
But you needn't be anxious. I will
tell you by the first or second day's
post, this coming week, exactly what I
am doing, and why. These books are
really bought for the Sheffield or other
St. George's Museums; and I, with
one foot—and perhaps one knee—in

the grave, have only to catalogue and describe them. But, I daresay, I shall be able to stand on one leg, and keep my head above ground yet awhile;— only you really needn't care how much I'm worth at the Bank—where the wild thyme does *not* blow !

Yes, I *was mort*ified—*death*ified— by your never having seen those Scott letters ! I thought everybody read the *Nineteenth Century*, and that these papers on *Fiction* would be matter of gossip all over Town ! Such my vanity ! and I haven't heard a word of them from any human soul !

Ever your affectionate (but much crushed),

J. R[USKIN].

LETTER XXXIV.

BRANTWOOD,
CONISTON, LANCASHIRE.
May 17th, 1881.

MY DEAR ELLIS,

I am exceedingly delighted by your kindness in sending me these drawings. I shall send over to the station this afternoon for them : and, as I doubt not they will be there at latest by the six train, I shall be able to examine and dispatch again to-morrow, quite easily.*

---

* The drawings referred to were two designs or cups or chalices — supposed to be by Holbein, and so described by Mr. Reid, Keeper of the Prints at the British Museum.

They were included in an immense illustrated copy of Walpole's *Painters* —enlarged into 18 vols. folio, by a Mr Bull, a friend of Walpole's Mr. A. C. Swinburne had inherited the volumes, with others of a like kind.

I can tell Holbein at a glance, and
so, it seemed to me, could Mr. Reid,
whose judgment I have found fine and
trustworthy beyond any person's I
know, in his own branch of Art—
(more's the pity! he got hold of the
best sepia drawing by Turner in the
world!) And if *he wished* to bid, I've
no doubt the drawings are all right,
and that I shall return them with *carte
blanche* to you.

I shall keep the lovely edition of
Sidonis,* with sincerest thanks for all
your good help lately. I am daily in
expectation of the finish of the lawyers
with a bit of business, which ended,
you shall have cheque for *St.
Ronan's,†* and all, at once.

They were sold at Sotheby's in 1880, and bought by
Mr. Ellis for £1,800. The volumes were then broken up,
and the contents sold by auction as separate drawings
and prints. The two drawings in question were bought by
Mr. W. Mitchell, a well-known collector, who esteemed
them to be genuine examples of Holbein. They were
probably re-sold with the rest of his drawings at Berlin,
about 1890 or 1891.

    * *Sidonii Apollinaris Opera*, folio.

    † The autograph MS. of *St. Ronan's Well.*

I am doing as good work as ever, *I* think, at *Amiens.** The second chapter will have some bits more in the old *Stones of Venice* manner, than I've troubled myself to write lately.

Ever affectionately and gratefully yours,

J. RUSKIN.

* *The Bible of Amiens,* Chap. 2, *Under the Drachenfels,* published in *Dec.* 1881.

LETTER XXXV.

BRANTWOOD,
CONISTON, LANCASHIRE.
[1881.]

DEAR ELLIS,

I only send you the *last* of the Scott papers;* for I can't find the first : and the middle ones won't read right without it (the readers, fool enough, complained that it *would .'*). Please you must get *for me* —and read, if you like, first—Numbers 43, *Sept.* 1880,

42, *Aug.* 1880, and, I believe, 40, *June*, 1880. But please find out; and send me *this one* back when you've read what you *can* of it

---

* *Fiction, Fair and Foul*, which appeared in the *Nineteenth Century*.

- and the others with the *first*, when you've read what you *like* of it,—which I hope you will, some.

Ever your affectionate,

J. R[USKIN]

LETTER XXXVI.

Brantwood,
Coniston, Lancashire.
[1881.]

My Dear Ellis,

Please send me these Carlyle *Reminiscences.* I'm up reading them now, and that rascally article of Mrs. Wedgwood's has put my bristle up,— and I must give her a hiding—somewhere—short and sweet. The comic thing is, that the three sentences of Carlyle's she quotes above, are the only ones worth printing in the entire article. That on Coleridge is superb.

Please (to save me the trouble of writing another note) can you, in regular way of business, get a copy of my

Prout *Notes* with illustrative photos,
from over the way. I gave mine
away, thinking I'd half a dozen—but
no such luck.

Ever your affectionate,

J. R[uskin].

LETTER XXXVII.

DEAR PAPA ELLIS,

I am so very glad to know you like that *Fors*, especially that part of it. I know that my illnesses have greatly weakened the physical grasp of the brain, so that I can never more write things rich in thought like the preface to *Grimm ;* but I believe the general balance and truth of thought are still safe—or even safer than before the strain.

Yes, there *is* a new world coming— God knows what ! But there's a handful of good seed coming up, every here and there.

If these books of mine would be any good at Whitelands College, send them there. If not, get what price they'll fetch.

Ever affectionately yours,

J. RUSKIN.

F. S. Ellis, Esq.

LETTER XXXVIII.

BRANTWOOD,
CONISTON, LANCASHIRE.
July 7th, 1883.

DEAR ELLIS,

I am so ashamed of never having answered your delightful letters—but I've been more busy than is good for me, necessarily, as one always finds if one is busy at all. And then I did not know you were going to stay so long at the country place.

I am very happy in your patience with the Scott papers,—very happy in the loan of your lovely Missal,—very happy in being able to covet missals, and take pride in my own work, once more. And very happy shall I be when I can shake hands again in that delightful library and chat-room of yours.

And this is all I can say to day—else I shall miss the post again !

Ever your affectionate and grateful,

J. RUSKIN.

LETTER XXXIX.

—

BRANTWOOD,
CONISTON, LANCASHIRE.
June 1st, 1884.

DEAR ELLIS,

May I give the name of the writer of enclosed bit * for next *Fors* correspondence? It would be of weight in driving down the sentence about Scott, which is of extreme importance and value.

I send you an old book, which has been inherited by my washerwoman!

* This was a printed extract from a letter of Mr. Ellis's regarding the condition of a certain English village. The consent asked was freely given, though with a modification of some of the expressions Mr. Ellis had originally used.

Can you impress her mind with rever-
ence for literature by giving her a few
shillings for it?

Ever affectionately yours,

J. R[USKIN].

LETTER XI.

BRANTWOOD,
CONISTON, LANCASHIRE.
June 6th, 1884.

DEAR ELLIS,

I am so very sorry you have been ill, I never dreamed of such a thing. Take care now ; I shall be anxious till you write again to say you're going on well.—To think of my having forgiven the Hamilton business like this ! *

I'll cut out all the vice.—Your last letter still more valuable—is, I think, quite safe and general.

Your loving,
J. R[USKIN].

* Mr. Ruskin was, or professed to be, grievously hurt and offended with Mr. Ellis for having negociated the purchase of the Hamilton Manuscripts for the Berlin Museum.

LETTER XLI.

BRANTWOOD,
CONISTON, LANCASHIRE.
February 3rd, 1885.

DEAR ELLIS,

We're both brutes for never asking
after each other,—and you wait a bit
before you thank me for being the
first to speak, for it's forced by a bit of
business, which will be best told you
by my secretary. Don't look down
upon her for being a girl. She's got
nice business ways, and will save you
a lot of trouble in writing gossip ; and,
besides, tell *me* all about *you*, and you
all about me, -and the business con-
cerns her a little. It's about some
old Bibles of her uncle's. Will you

please write to her, Miss ANDERSON, 46, Warwick Gardens, and tell her where she could see you,—or will Mr. White kindly make an appointment for her if Mr. Ellis is out of town.

Meantime, if you care to know it, I'm pretty well, and pretty busy, and rather pleased with my work ; and am,

Affectionately yours,

J. RUSKIN.

F. S. Ellis, Esq.

LETTER XLII.

BRANTWOOD,
CONISTON, LANCASHIRE.
January 18th, 1886.

DEAR ELLIS,

Your pathetic note has lain beside me. I could not at first answer, for I was very ill,—but this sweet spring sunlight on the moor cheers me, and makes me feel as if we both might rejoice in spring days again. But I am recovering very slowly from the depression of this last illness, and can only say, that I am ashamed of having been sad.

But please write and tell me you also are gaining, and what the illness was which has taken you from the work in which you seemed so happy.

Ever affectionately yours,

J. RUSKIN.

F. S. Ellis, Esq.

ERRATUM.

Page 51, line 3—for *Packet* read *Packed.*

INDEX.

INDEX.

Privately Printed: 1892.

www.ingramcontent.com/pod-product-compliance
Lightning Source LLC
Chambersburg PA
CBHW032156010726
47493CB00008BA/2721